Intense Emotion

From Kingston to the Country and Back

Two Different Worlds

Orville Hutchinson

© 2017 Orville Hutchinson
All rights reserved.

ISBN: 1548963305
ISBN-13: 978-1548963309
Library of Congress Control Number: 2017911307
LCCN Imprint Name: Create space Independent Publishing Platform North Charleston South Carolina

Table of Contents

Title Page ....

Copyright ....

Table of Content ....

Acknowledgment.............................

Read This First................................

Introduction... 1

Two Different Worlds........................ 3

The Passion 9

Who Is Dane?.......................................18

Chain of Events 27

My Sister and I................................... 33

The Good Samaritan 38

The Unseen 40

There Was Hope................................ 53

The Acceptance 58

Embarrassing moment..................... 61

My Cousins and I 64

The Secret Passage **68**

A Hungry Boy **76**

The Clash **82**

Conclusion **86**

Glossary.. *88*

Acknowledgment

I would like to thank and acknowledge the people who influence and inspired me to write this book. I'm also thankful for the experience I had in the country with my relatives in order for me to tell this story. I give thanks to God for his supreme generosity in enabling me to complete this book. I would like to first say that I appreciate my immediate family: My wife, whom I adore so much, for always being there for me with words of encouragement and full support; her professional criticism helped me to view things in more than one way. My son, who challenges me with his unexpected questions from time to time, keeps me in perspective, knowing that I have him to answer to.

I am also thankful to the International College of the Cayman Islands for offering the educational opportunity for me to re-educate myself, which gave me the wisdom and inspiration to write this book. Also to everyone who believed in me supported me through this chapter in my life and who never showed any sign of doubt in any of my endeavors. To the people who have been through similar experiences, and also kids who are facing this chapter in their lives. You are one of the main reasons why this book was written with the thought of my past, which I use to strengthen, guide, and set my standard to be the man I am today.

Read This First

I extend my gratitude to you for finding the time to read this book. To whomever this book reaches, I hope that it touches your heart in ways that will make you think before judging, as well as giving you the understanding of how to approach any situation. Once you begin reading this book, you will get to see that many who have shared or are going through similar situations might not be as fortunate as I was.

This means that you have the opportunity to make a difference in someone's life in a positive way. Every day when we rise, there is a lot to be thankful for, because I have a strong belief that everything happens in life for a purpose. You are not reading this book in vain; there is a special reason why this book reached you. I take it that you are of good intention and you will make this story create better where it's needed.

If you don't have any emotions, this book is not for you. However, you can just hand it to someone who you think will be more interested in this kind of story, as I trust that not everyone has the same desire. As for you who are willing to make a positive change in life for the greater good, continue to read this book. You will see that attention and love can improve any situation. This book will make you go to your inner self and let you want to show that you care. Know that I write this book to shed light on situations that happened and might still be happening in our society.

Here I come to you with this story, hoping that after you read it, it can help you to make a difference in a good way before it is too late. So if you should see a child or even an adult looking lost or needing someone to talk to, see if you can find the time to make that save. You might just be that person's savior. Even if he or she doesn't say thanks to you, don't worry about it. One day that person will come to the understanding that what you did impact his or her life, and for that he or she will be grateful.

Introduction

Intense emotion is a psychological behavior, the way in which a person, organism, or group responds to a specific set of conditions. This book is talking about my intense emotion as a boy. I had a rough childhood, which had a strong impact on my life and created a distance between me and my relatives. Even though I wasn't the worst child growing up in the world, I felt like I was and also felt like I was alone in the world. This made me feel like an outcast, which had me in a depressed mood most of the time. I didn't even think that I would survive to tell this story.

Some information in this book might be disturbing to you as the reader. My grandpa would say to us grandkids at bedtime he would shout from the other room "Pray before you go to your bed." My advice to you would be the same as Dada (Grandfather): pray before you enter on this reading journey.

In Kingston, we would speak proper English, but in the rural district we would speak patois, which is Jamaican Creole, so there are some words that I will have to define for you. I will tell you about my world and what revolved around it in the first twelve years of my life, what I was passionate about, and why this book is titled *Intense Emotion*. I will talk about the good times and the bad times that have motivated me to be the person I am today.

Two Different Worlds

Two different worlds: it makes me question what my life would be like if I hadn't gone to live in the country. My life in Kingston with my family was a life that I had to accept regardless of what happened; for example, the beatings and resentment with my mother and father were all I knew. However, the other world I was taken to when I went to my relatives in the country was a whole new experience of life at a tender age. This is why I call them two different worlds; it seems impossible to combine both worlds. Looking at each world from the outside, it seems to fill one with uncertainty, not knowing which world is better. I was born a Kingstonian, not knowing what it is like to be born in the rural district, so of course, when one looks at the other world, the assumption arises that the other world would be better.

Because the master of understanding is experience, one without experience is lacking knowledge. Now I have become a man of understanding and knowledge, which enables me to compose this literature from one world to another. Because I have gained the experience and the knowledge to understand both worlds, I am able to share this story with you. The intensity of my experience brought knowledge to me, and the emotion brings me to express this story.

But are these worlds really that different? A city bwoy, that's what they would call me just because I was born in Kingston. To the other world, the city would be a dream world, but I just couldn't see why it was a big deal to leave the country and move to the city. But when I moved from the city and went to live in the country, I understood why. The conditions were totally different. The rural district was mostly forest, mountains, rivers, and farmlands, and the houses, the kitchens, and restrooms were not joined to the house.

The city had high-rise buildings, paved roads, streetlights, and more transportation, and technology was everywhere. I understand why a person from the rural district would want to migrate to the city. But that was in the 1980s, and as I became mature, I started to understand the luxury of the rural district, which is nature itself.

Nature, the landscape was magnificent, rivers, ponds, plants, produce, animal and so much more. In the rural district where it was custom in those days when everyone would drink the water from the spring which was unfiltered also when it rain there were tanks and drums that would be filled with water from the sky. The air you breathe was light clean and unpolluted and the food was organic. With that said I guess it can be argued which world is better.

In the rural district, there wasn't much interference from the city life to influence, change of habits which made things run smooth. No one would notice that another have a gas stove to cook are bake in an oven. So it was common for woodfire to be used in those days for to cooking or baking. Also, there weren't any water running out of a facet we didn't have face basin, kitchen sink or running shower. You would have to use a bath pan or go to the river to take a bath with the natural mineral water with no chlorine. It was natural, most of what we would consume was mostly produced by the villagers except for rice, flour, and tin-goods which we didn't even consume much of.

Coffee, mint leaf, and fever grass just to name a few we would pick fresh off the farmland and cocoa that was used to make hot chocolate tea. Tubers (these are plants with notable tuberous roots such as sweet potatoes, yams, and cassava), fresh fruits, vegetable, and meat also cornmeal that we would get from our own corn and so much more. In the rural district those days there wasn't any shortage of organic food. Also, the people were manner-able everyone would have the courtesy to say good morning, good day, good evening and good night. Those people would show care and respect for each other. Farmers would help each other both male and female; the children would go to school and do other chores.

Now consider the alternative wherein the city life is way different everywhere you go its mostly manmade structure of concrete and steel, artificial plants while the nature that was are diminishing. Polluted air and over chlorinated water this is the city life. But for someone who has no knowledge of the farming lifestyle, this was a lot to take on at that tender age in my life. We were walking from school one day and as we were about to go around the corner on the hill which had 4ft wall on the left side of the road. I heard a loud unusual sound I was frightened to the point where I jump over the wall into the gully.

My cousin who was born in the country started to laugh at me and then came to comfort me telling me that it's okay, it is just a donkey braying. I cried and it was just because I had never heard a sound like that before. But back when I was in the city the loud sounds I was used to were gunshots as when the shooting started whoever I was staying with would put the children under the bed or tell us to lie on the floor. Firecracker was another loud noise that I was used to in the city but that donkey bray scares the tears out of me.

City live that's me and I was used to this lifestyle with my manmade structure and relics. But then I was taken to a whole new world a place I had never heard of before in the country where I had to adjust, learn and adapt. With unusual faces and custom, I must say there was no way, shape or form I was prepared for what I was about to get into. If I was to debate on which world was the best at that day and age in my life it would be difficult to choose. Because of the way my parent treated me as a child in the city raising me and then took me to the country and left me in a whole new environment without sticking around to show me how to handle the new path.

The Passion

This book is title *Intense Emotion* because of the experiences of my youth. I don't know how I survived, but I did, and I guess it's because I am supposed to be here to tell this story, among other things. I question myself to try and justify what happened to me as a child, mainly from the age of seven to when I was twelve years old. It was my fault that my life was so hard, as everyone thinks that their burden is the heaviest when all I wanted was my family: my mother, father, and sister.

I always wanted to do music from the time I was a young boy. I like the entertainment world. I guess it was just the way everyone could relate to it. People from all walks of life just connected to the beat, and I was one with that passion. *"Mi a-tell yuh, Mon"* (I'm telling you, man), I always wanted to do music as a child growing up. Oh, I love entertaining. When I was about nine years old I can remember I was acting and doing music —I was always doing some form of entertainment, whether it was making rhymes or acting like I was on television. Back then entertaining was all I would think about. I was always excited when it came to the performing arts.

But it wasn't anything serious to me. I would only act for whoever was around me, and then I would be spitting rhymes over beats for my cousins. I can remember it like it was yesterday; my uncle had bought a pink double-deck cassette tape player that we hid and used when no adults were around. You see, in those days, kids didn't have the freedom as such, because the elders would ask you if you were an idiot. This was in the late part of the 1980s. Some of the elders back then were narrow-minded when it came to educating children about what they could become in life. In those days and that district, the only way of life they knew was farming.

I don't want to go too much into details about their parenting right now, as it will draw us away from what I was so passionate about entertaining. Yes, I remember my cousins used to say, *"Dane good, eh, Mon" Ehm a act Lakka eh people dem in a eh TV show,"* (Dane is good, he is acting just like the actors in the movies on the TV) but as I said, it didn't mean anything because I wasn't taught that I could make a career being an actor or a stage performer. So I would go on and kept playing around, acting and spitting lyrics. Let's get back to the cassette tape deck; when my cousins would play the songs on a cassette, even though there were lyrics playing over the beat, I could still ride the rhythm.

'Yeah, Mon,' that's what we would call it: "ride the rhythm." Oh boy, those days were nice, when we were just being ourselves. So I would make my own songs about things that used to happen in the district. Yes, I was an on-the-spot lyricist. I could chat lyrics from morning till night. We were young and innocent, and that made all the difference. Back then we didn't even have a microphone. You would have thought that I would grow up to be the entertainer in the family. I guess you will find out as you continue to read this book. Anyhow, we were just living in the moment, and that was all that mattered to us. We were so happy.

You would think that I would have grown up with the same passion and pursued a career as an entertainer. It all would depend on what you classify as an accomplishment in your own sense of accomplishing something. For me, being accomplished just knows I had an opportunity to do or be something and tried at it, while you might not see it that way. You might think that if doing something isn't profitable to provide for you or your family it means that you are not accomplished, as it is not deemed highly. In that case, I wouldn't argue your terms because we would be of two different levels of satisfaction.

Well, let's find out what happened. Did I grow up with the same passion, or did the flair die? The question arises, and we will all know the answer sometime in this book. But for now, let's get into a little detail about the little boy, Orville Hutchinson, a.k.a. Dane. The truth of the matter is that this moment lasted between the ages of nine and twelve; yes, through the whole three years, and it did go on through the innocence of the time.

At age of seven, I didn't have a mother and father love and support, as my dad had taken me to the country and left me there. Not that I am using that as an excuse to get out of any situation. It must have hurt my granddad's feelings because all I did was cry and say that I would run away, so he didn't talk to me much. He would only say little things to make me smile, knowing that he was there for me, just like how he was there for the other grandkids in every way.

As time went by and I got more comfortable, I would start to do things with my cousins. We would smoke dry leaves and act like adults. That was the first time I would participate in such an act; however, it wouldn't stop there. We would want more, and we went for it, but this time it wasn't the ordinary dry leaves from the trees. We would wait until we are alone. When Dada left the house, we would go through his bedside table drawer, as he would keep some marijuana hidden in it. We would have a ball, using a brown paper bag to roll the marijuana in and lighting it, like the elders that we saw smoke.

A (spliff) that's what we call marijuana that is rolled up in a piece of paper in Jamaica. I went to the country in the second grade as a straight (A) student from Pembroke hall basic school. But when I start to make new friends in the country I become less of a straight (A) student. Because even though I was an unwanted child in the city my grades were great. Because I had a teacher who would spend time with me, I can remember how she would stand over me hold my hand with my pencil while she helps me to write on the line and stay within the margin. Even though I can't remember her name I also remember she would teach me to spell by breaking up words into syllables.

In the country I didn't care as I felt alone, but when I start to make friends at the Olive River all age school. It felt good as I got accepted by others who made me felt like I was wanted. So we would start to do things like skipping school and for me, this was the first time I have ever done these things. In Jamaica, we would say (skull school/class) this would mean that we didn't go to school or show up in class. This bad habit started to become a pursuit for me and I must say it was to my liking.

So, of course, I would dress up in my uniform like I was going to school and didn't show up for class find a spot where I knew that no adults would be at that time because teachers would be in class, nurses and doctors would be in the clinic and farmers would be on the farm. This was when I would go at a spot behind the church and write in my book something like I was in class at school. I taught I was smart by dating my book with the subject and write some notes. This was for if I reach home and mama asks to see in my book I would have something to show her.

As dada usually busies on the farm he didn't have any time to checkbooks. I realize that this was easy putting on my uniform leave the house go do what I wanted and not show up in class I felt good. While we weren't in school we would go to the river without thinking that we could get hurt, it was me and my two other friends' one was Andrew and the other was called Noisy. All the time when I went to the river with my friends I would sing and act, and getting something to eat wasn't a problem. This river was located in the middle of a banana farm and we would have dozens of ripe bananas to eat and our lunch money we would put together and buy bulla cake and those were some nice bulla cake I would like the ones with the ginger flavor.

It wasn't long before we got caught and we did suffer the consequence which made me never skull-school again. I adjusted and adapt with my peers in the country which help me become comfortable in my surrounding. But I learned that by doing wrong, acting brave and feeling free felt good and gave me my independence. However, with all the tricks, I had learned like how to lie and cover for each other by trying to get myself out of trouble just became a whole new me in a whole new different world. Because as the old saying goes, "when you tell a lie thinking that it will get you out of trouble you are only making things worse for yourself.

So when I was *skulling* (Skipping) school and not showing up in class believing that I was doing something good I came to realize that I wasn't. Out of all the wrongs I was doing I learned my most valuable lesson was never to do wrong and believe that good will come from it.

Who Is Dane?

I was born on July 1, 1977, at 4:45 a.m. My birthplace was the Victoria Jubilee Hospital (VJH), Kingston, Jamaica, and I was named Orville O'Neil Stephens Hutchinson. My mother was Eva Veronica Montaque, my father was Basil Raymond Hutchinson, and my sister was named Ann Marie Hutchinson. Who knows what the future will be? If we did it would be scary, wouldn't it? I don't have a lot of memories as to what my life was like or even what my parents' lives were like. What I remember was that I use to attend Pembroke Hall Infant Center. I was also an *A*-grade student at the top of my class. I also remember walking from Pembroke Hall School to my home in Gregory Park, under the age of seven which was 6.3 miles

I know there is no manual on how to raise a child, however, the way my dad play his part of raising me as a child in the little time he had me with him wasn't a way I would raise my children. Speaking now as a father of two sons, he wasn't close to being a father. I do remember some of the times when I use to go visit my father at his house with him and my step-mother her child was always there living and I was just a visitor. That was in the 80s when marijuana was the highlight of everything. But it was also illegal which make it more interested for one to sneak and used in their privacy without getting caught.

My dad was a big marijuana user and when I would go to his house to visit I would remember his friends would shout "Head"! Just a nickname he picks up from them instead of calling him by his birth name. Head was short for bighead. Even though I don't believe that his friends even knew his birth name. It's sometimes like that in Jamaica where nicknames are mostly used. Another thing that would happen was he would use marijuana in my presence as if he grooming me to become a pothead/marijuana user like him. As to this day, I don't understand what he was trying to accomplish by doing that. Maybe he thought that by grooming me to become a ganja man it would have made me more educated or become wealthy.

The question is, was he wrong or right, was he being a good father to want his son the only son he had also the child that he said wasn't his to become a ganja man. Personally, I would say that he wasn't showing good parenting skill. What he would do was take me when he was about to smoke and put me to sit in front of him while he would role his spliff or load his challis so I can see and know how to do so myself. Then he would light it up and I would watch him inhale the smoke as if everything was depending on that moment and he was the savior. So confident having a child in the midst of his smoking ritual not even thinking that second-hand smoke is one of the leading cause of lungs cancer.

He would take a puff and for every puff, he would take he would exhale and blow the smoke into my face. That was his way of grooming me to be like him even though he said that I wasn't his child. But I can remember there was a cutting board with ganja and he would treat it like his life was depending on it. How precious the marijuana was because it was more important to him than I was. Because the only time I was able to mean something to him was when he would get to puff and exhale the smoke of the marijuana in my face.

I can't remember him ever opening a book with me showing me how to solve an equation, spell a word, teaching me the alphabet or how to survive in the world. But when the smoking ritual was over I would just go about my business or playing with my friends because I wasn't important anymore. As to my recollection of memories, I was busy in my own world, attending school and playing dally house, yes, that's what we called it when our parents would leave us kids alone for a few hours and we played house.

This was one of my favorite games because I got to be the dad. What happened was that a boy would play Dad and a girl would play Mom. We would also play hide-and-seek and ring games, too. My favorite ring game was There Is a Brown Girl in the Ring cause I would get to dance with the brown girl in the ring. My sister, Ann Marie, a.k.a. Janette, couldn't stand me, as I used to lock her out of the house when I played dally house. I don't remember much about my living conditions because we used to move so much. I just could not keep track of all the places.

Because my mother and father were separated, we moved from house to house. This would cause a lot of neglect for us children because they weren't civil parents. They would spite each other, and as a result of that, we would end up as subjects. Back and forth we would end up going, from our mother's to our father's house. It wasn't a joy ride. And the fact that I was the unwanted child would even make it tougher for me. I didn't understand why my life was like that, but they were my parents, so whatever their choice was would be my fate.

Olympic Gardens is in the parish of Saint Andrew and is located in Jamaica - some 3 mi or 5 km North-West of Kingston, the country's capital city.I do not remember much of when I was living at 102 Olympic Way, right by the bridge on the main road. I know this address because it is the one on my birth certificate, and Mom told me that it was my birthplace. Also, one of my cousins wouldn't wake up one morning; she died in her sleep they said, and she was buried beside the house. As an adult, I went there to look for my uncle, and I could see the grave, as it is old and falling apart. I believe that even now my uncle still lives there with his family.

I use to have fears as a young boy, one of which was of an ornament of an Arawak Indian face. But never I ever imagine that I would be separated from my parents care. It happened and it was terrible, I use to have a nightmare of a liquid stuff that would make me sick to my stomach even after I woke up. It was like different color oil paint just gushing nonstop. That would let me fear sleep as I would rather lay awake with my eyes open because I didn't want to enter that spooky world of liquid nightmare.

This was something I use to keep to myself as I wasn't brought up in an environment to share my fears with my mom or dad so to go and talk to them about my dreams or nightmare that was a no. Another thing is going to sleep and having that moment where I was walking on a hard level plane field and out of nowhere, I started to go down in quicksand. At first, I would jump out of my sleep scared, afraid and lonely. As the quicksand dream became more frequent I just let myself under the sand and watch as I slowly travel through the quicksand. Somehow I was breathing fine until the fear kicked in and I started to choke and jump out of my sleep.

Those nightmares were scary but the scariest one of all my nightmare was the one when I was living in the country. Wow, it felt as if my heart was palpitating. And for some odd reason, the nightmare of the liquid oil paint was the one that seems like it would just keep following me everywhere I go. It wasn't until I went to my bed in the country and dreamt that I was walking from the house where I lived which was under the hill.

So I dreamt I was walking over the hill and as I reach to the corner of the hill which was the darkest part of the journey at the point right before I would reach to where the light was, I would come to face with a shadow of a big monster that would bounce left to right of the road and block me from passing so I could never reach the light. The light which I could only get a glimpse of this nightmare was the scariest one of all my nightmares.

As I kept on having that nightmare I realize that I could not keep running away from this monster. I had to get to my destination and if I wanted to reach there the only way was by that big scary monster. It reaches the point where I didn't see that monster anymore and I would make it to the light around the corner. Still, that was half of my journey and standing under that street light looking at where I am supposed to go just seems like an impossible journey.

This is the house where I was taken after being born at the Victoria Jubilee Hospital.

Chain of Events

I also remember the address 32 Dennis Avenue, Gregory Park, Portmore P.O, Saint Catherine, because it was a house that my father rented. It was on about an acre of land with at least four huge mango trees and several jelly trees, soursop trees, star apple trees, sweetsop trees, and guinep trees. The house was one bedroom and a living room, but in the living room, he had a bed as well as a stove. That living room was a bedroom, kitchen, and living room in one. We had to take baths outside because the house didn't have a bathroom; the toilet was separate and was used by everyone who had rented a house on the premises.

There were more houses on the premises, and when you walked down to the back of the land, there was a horse stable behind us. This is what we would call a tenement yard. There was a little shop where you could get little things to buy at any hour of the day or night. The shop used to sell sweets, and I used to love those sweets. We called them Busta-sweeties. Every cent I had used to go to Busta-sweeties; that was one of my weaknesses as a child.

The ruins of the house I use to live in as a child in Gregory Park Jamaica

I lived there for a while with my dad and my stepmother. I used to refer to my stepmother as Aunty Nola. My stepmother also had a daughter, whom I knew as Mishka. I remember my stepsister because when I used to get my food, she would take away my meat, eat it off, and give me back the bone. My stepsister and stepmother were big in body, so I would stay out of their way. I remember that in those days, I just couldn't do anything right in my father's sight. For the least of things, he would beat me with this big leather belt. I suppose it made him feel like more of a man.

When anything bad happened to me, I wouldn't tell him because I was afraid that he would still put the blame on me. This made me feel as if I was an unwanted child. I remember there was an ornament in the house, the head of an Arawak Indian painted in black and white. I was afraid of it, but no one cared. One evening while I was on my way home from school this man was riding a bicycle, and I will remember this to my grave because of what happened. I saw him riding toward me from a distance. I tried to get out of the rider's way, but he was still pursuing me.

If I walked over to the left side of the road, he would ride his bike over to the left side of the road. So, I walked back over to the right side of the road, and he would ride back over to the right side of the road. I just couldn't escape this rider. He hit me with the bicycle, rode over me, and left the scene like it was nothing. I was a child, and I wasn't in any position to defend myself, so I got up, brushed off my school uniform, and headed home. Apparently no one had seen the incident to intervene; furthermore, my home was about three houses away.

But of course, I didn't say anything to my father, as he wasn't someone I felt comfortable confiding in. I felt alone and afraid of my own father. I remember one incident where the rain was pouring down, and I was happy, so I got myself a big towel and tied it around my shoulders like a cape. I ran out into the rain, shouting, "Superman!" Who did I run into? My Kryptonite was my father, and I did get a beating from him with that big leather belt. So, of course, I didn't go to him when the cyclist deliberately ran me over, afraid that my father would have blamed me anyway. Anyhow, that was then, and here I am alive and well, telling the story of my life because now I have the strength and health to do so.

My Sister and I

What do I remember about my sister and me? Not much; we didn't spend much time together as brother and sister growing up. But I can tell you about a train incident that happened while we were leaving our father's house to go to our mother's. There was this house that I don't remember the address, but that's where I used to play dally house and lock her out. We stayed with our father on the weekends, and then he would send us back to our mother throughout the week. We stayed with Mommy during the week because she took us to school. I guess that Daddy didn't think that he should have any part in getting us to school.

That weekend we had stayed at Dad's house, and it was time to go back home to our house with Mom. It was an early Sunday evening, and the night was coming down. We headed out to the Gregory Park bus terminus to catch the bus home, but the train station was at the same location. I believe that responsible parents should take their children to the bus stop, especially children who are under seven years old.

No, not our father—he didn't bring us to the bus stop to make sure that we got on the right bus. Daddy just gave us our lunch money and bus fare, and then sent us home. We did make it home, but not before the unthinkable happened. Take into consideration that my sister is one year older than I am before you judge us in this situation. I would think that since she was the eldest, I would have to obey whatever she said. Well, I guess she wanted to try the same thing I wanted to try because I knew her well. If she hadn't wanted to do it, she would have said no. Anyhow, we both did it; even though it was my idea, we went for it together.

While standing at the bus terminus waiting for the bus to come, I was getting impatient. I saw that the train had come and suggested to Janette, "Let's go take the train." So the train we did take. We were excited to go on the train. The train ride was nice, but we realized that we had been on the train for a while. That's when we asked a lady who was a passenger on the train where we were and told her where we were going. We were lost. Immediately I began to worry because I knew that we would be in trouble, and worst of all, it was all because of me.

Then my sister and I started to cry because we only had enough money to take the bus home. To ride the train was more expensive, so we took some of our lunch money to make up the difference for the train ticket. I started to ask my sister, "What we are going to do? How we are going get home?" Then my sister started to blame me, saying, "This is your fault," and I knew it was the truth, and that made me even more worried and scared.

The ruins of the train station where my sister and I took the train and got lost.

The Good Samaritan

As we cried on the train, a lady saw us and noticed what was going on. She was so nice, but I could see that confused look on her face. She must have been wondering if she should go out of her way to help us get home or take us to the nearest police station. Oh my, that poor lady stood there with us as if she didn't know what to do. She must have felt as if she had taken the world upon her shoulders because we were complete strangers to her. But what saved us was the fact that we were children. She questioned us, and we told her where we were going, and she took us home and handed us over to our mother.

I just want to take the time now to thank that lady for her courageous and compassionate action in taking us home. I don't know her name, and if I saw her now, I would just walk past her without knowing it was her. But even though I don't know her, she was a Good Samaritan, a godsend to us that night. Thank you for taking us home to our mother. I really appreciate what you did.

The lady handed us over to our mother, and oh, I was so happy to see her, thinking that she would be pleased to know that someone had gone out of their way to bring her children home to her. No, no—not my mother. At the top of her voice, she shouted. I knew that tone. She went straight for the mop stick and beat me without mercy as if I were a criminal. My sister got off scot-free. I felt like the lady wanted to stop her from beating me, but my mother took me inside.

The Unseen

The unseen: a path that I can't tell you in words how it happened, but all I know is that it happened. I ended up in the country. I had no knowledge of how it was planned. Neither of my parents talked to me about my destiny, or what they had decided to do with me. Irrelevant—that's how they must have seen me, without thinking that I would grow up to question their responsibilities as parents. Even though my parents had me back and forth, as if neither of them wanted me to be his or her responsibility, it was still ok to me because they were my parents. It was bad but tolerable when my parents treated me badly in any way, but when a relative or a stranger does the same; it feels ten times worse to me.

When my father left me in the country, it took me a while to adapt. Even though I was with my relatives, I felt more alone than when I was living back and forth with my mother and father.

Sometime in 1984, I ended up in the parish of Trelawney. This much I remember: My dad took me to the country once to visit and then took me back to Kingston. Then he took me back to the same parish in the country and left me on my uncle's veranda steps. I had no clue what was happening, so when he left, I spent some time at my uncle's place, and then my uncle brought me to my granddad's house.

This was up in the hills of Trelawney, a place called Hill Sixty, up on a mountain overlooking the green luscious valley, with rivers running, and the water as cold as ice. When I woke up in the mornings, fog would cover the road as if the sky had come down and touched the mountaintop. I could smell Mama making breakfast over the wood fire, and I can remember hearing the crackling sound of the burning wood. The aroma would make me discern what was for breakfast. I could tell if I was having freshly picked mint tea with fried dumplings or velvety rich cocoa tea that was picked, dried, parched, and beaten down to a powdery perfection, served with blue-Drawers pudding. Blue Drawers otherwise called "Duckunoo" or tie leaf - this is a starchy green banana base boiled pudding. It's made with banana, sweet potatoes, coconut milk and spices with some sugar and sometimes raisins. This is all mixed together and wrap in banana leaf or foil and then drop into boiling water.

My uncle's name is Mr. Phillip Hutchinson; everyone called him Uncle or Presho. I have no idea why they nicknamed him Presho, but it was a popular name for him. When he returned from overseas, he was the talk of the town. His friends would come to see him. I remember one of his friends came by to look for him on a big motorbike. My uncle went on the bike and tried to ride it, but the bike was so powerful it flew over a ditch with him.

Granddad's name was Mr. Ferdinand Hutchinson, a.k.a. Dada, or best known to others in the district as Mass/Dah Kerdy. My grandfather was married to my step-grandmother, Mrs. Enid Hutchinson, known to some as Mama or Mrs. Dally in that district. There were also five cousins: Sandra Smith and Patrick Smith, a.k.a. Dave, who are brother and sister; Nadine

Baker and Jeffrey Lewis, a.k.a. Godfrey, another brother and sister; and Dawn Thompson, who was not family by blood, but she was living with us, so I call her my cousin. Oh yes, and myself, Orville O'Neil Stephen Hutchinson, a.k.a. Dane, the only grandchild in the bunch who had Hutchinson as a surname, but yet I was the outcast and disowned. I was added to the pack of grandkids that my grandpa and step-grandma took in and raised the best way they could, emotionally, financially, physically, and mentally,

 I was kind of the odd child, as my cousins were born in the country and I was born in Kingston, which classified me as a "city boy." Everything was harder for me because they were already seasoned in the country way of living. At the age of seven, they would be lifting up five-gallon buckets of water, putting them on their heads, and carrying them for miles at least twice a day. Not only that, but their knowledge of doing their chores were way more advanced than mine, like what to do and how it was to be done.

One thing was for sure: no one ever liked to go to the shop to buy anything. Why? Because the shop was so far, and you would have to climb a hill so steep you would be falling back while going over it. Then you would be timed, and when those old folks timed you, it was no joke. They would spit on the ground and tell you not to let it dry before you came back. And they took the whip out for you to see that they were serious. Once you saw that beating stick, it immediately put fear into you.

One thing I never forgot was my first day going to the farm field. I remember my cousins carrying buckets of water on their heads. I got a red plastic teacup and was totally oblivious to what was going to come. And it wasn't long before it happened. I had to manage my own bucket of water on my head, *Mon*. I was so vexed I must have spilled half the bucket before I reached my destination. I wasn't happy. I thought I would get away with spilling my water because I didn't want to carry it, I was wrong, as the less I carried, the more trips I would have to make to the spring until I carried the equivalent of my cousins.

I remember I used to cry day and night that I wanted to go back home to Kingston. I wanted my mother, I wanted my father, and little did I know that it was just the beginning. My cousins would try to make me feel a part of the family, but this life was nothing I was used to. The life I knew was just going to school, coming home, doing my homework, and playing with my friends. Now they had me carrying water, tending to animals, and farming. This was madness! All I could think of was how I could get out of this situation.

As time went by, how long could I continue to cry? The tears were dried up, but I was so unhappy. Trust me; I know what unhappiness feels like. When I went to bed, I would just pee the bed just because I thought they would send me back to Kingston. Then what came next was unexpected. As always, everyone knew what would happen to me besides me. But of course the fact is, for every action, there is a reaction, so here is what happened, because I had pee the bed, they put me on the floor to sleep.

So the floor became my bed for the rest of my stay in the country. On top of that, I can remember that my father only came two times to visit me, and I never saw my mother, not even once for the five years of my life that I was living in the country. So how did I become a full-fledged country boy? If I told you I knew how it happened, that would be a lie. All I can say is that the transition was made. I had to learn how to take the goats and tie them out in fresh pastures in the morning before school so they could get grass to eat. Then I would have to go back to get them when I came back from school in the evening. Since there were three boys, we would take turns with the handling of the animals.

I remember one evening it was my turn to go for the goats after school. I had a friend who lived next door to us, about five hundred yards away. His name was Andrew, and we also went to the same school. In that district, the chores for the kids were all the same, where boys would care for the animals, help out on the farm; provide wood for the fire that Mama used to cook with. On the other hand, the girls would sweep the yard, clean the house, and stay in the kitchen, where they would learn to cook. But both boys and girls would have to go to the spring and carry the same amount of water, as that water would be used for the cooking of food, washing of clothes, drinking, and other household uses.

It turns out Andrew and I had to do the same chore that evening. I don't remember the day, but it was in the evening after school and after we had dinner. We realized that we both had to go get the goats from the pasture. So we decided that we would go together. He said that we should go and get his goats first because they were closer than where I would go to get mine. I went with Andrew to get his goats, untied them, and gathered them. He then turned to me, saying that he couldn't follow me because it was getting late and his father would beat him. Once again, I didn't see that coming.

I was so upset, but I knew that I would get in trouble if I didn't go get my goats. The evening was getting dark, and I was a bit afraid because I knew that I had to go through this big banana farm, which was about three and a half miles. The owner had just passed away, and they were telling stories that his ghost was in the banana farm field, and the duppy (ghost) would take anybody who went in there away, so that made me afraid. I knew I had to go through that banana farm, so I built up my courage and went ahead alone, untied all my goats, gathered them, and began my journey home. Everything was going well about three miles into the journey. I was almost home. This was the first time in my life anything like this had ever happened to me.

The unthinkable happened. My goats were about five yards ahead of me when I saw this image floating to my right over in the bushes. It was like a woman in a wedding dress, but there was no face, and I don't remember seeing any feet. I started to cry instantly. We had a donkey called White Stallion, who was tied on the side of the road to the left of where I was witnessing this dramatic moment. So while the lady-like shape in this white gown floated across the road in front of me from my right to my left, I stood stiff, crying to the donkey. All I could say was, "Come, donkey, come." I said it until the image floated out of my sight. When it got out of the road and cleared my path, I must have taken off like a bullet from a gun. The next thing I remember is that I was in front of my cousins and Mama, telling them what I had seen.

On another evening, few weeks after my incident, I was heading home with my friend Andrew, talking and laughing and having a good time on the road. It was a little after nine in the night. Down the hill near our home, we both stopped and looked at each other, wondering if we were both seeing the same thing. Yes, we were. This time it wasn't one image, it was two, and this time it was two males floating across the road in front of us. But as soon as they crossed, we ran fast as lightning. We never spoke about it besides when I told my cousins what we saw.

I had to make myself comfortable, fit in with the rest of the kids, and face the reality that my dad had left me and he wasn't coming back anytime soon. The truth is, my eyes are filling with water, and I have a sad feeling in my heart after writing that sentence about my dad. But I will try to be strong in order to bring this story to life and make it be my guide in situations. I don't even remember the time period in which I became comfortable, but it must have been over a year or two because I went as far as to put a rope around my neck and tell them that I would kill myself, but my step-grandma called the rest of my cousins away and left me alone in my grief. Now I'm saying she must have known then that death wouldn't have come for me yet.

One day I was on the farm with a few elders and my cousins. We were planting peas, black-eyed red peas. The elder female and young ladies would drop the peas in the hole while the elder male and young men each dug holes with a hoe. The day was sunny and clear, and we were having a good time working, sweating, talking, singing, and planting. As usual for me, the unexpected had to happen. It was as if I wasn't feeling the sun while we were working, but all of a sudden, I started to feel the sun burning me. All because the conversation changed, and it was only about me.

The elders started off by complimenting me on how I was growing up as a good boy. Then another person said, "Yes, because when he had just gotten to the country, he didn't like it." So the whole conversation started to be about me. This is the shocking part of the conversation, the part that made it seem as if someone had turned up the sun on me and made me zone out for a moment. Someone said, "He is the dead stamp of his father," meaning I looked just like my dad. They elaborated, but I couldn't guess where they were taking the conversation. However, I knew that it was a good thing when someone told you that you looked like your father.

The person speaking seemed as if they have been waiting for a long time to utter these words to my ear. They said, "And his father was saying that he wasn't his child." Wow, not only did the sun felt hotter on me when I heard those words, but even the hoe that I was using felt heavier. As confused as I was with the whole situation, the only thing I heard after that was a reply "Yeah" and then everyone was silent for a while. I didn't even talk or play with anyone for the rest of the day.

There Was Hope

Hope came when I least expected it; I started to make a way out for myself by doing some farming. I would plant a little Irish potato, corn, red peas, and other things that kept me going. Funny little did I knew that my crops would yield something that I could sell and earn money to buy my own underwear and other necessities. My Uncle Phillip's wife I called her Aunty Liana would take my crop, as she was a food vendor who went to the market and sold food every weekend. She would take my Irish potatoes and red peas to the market, sell them, and buy things for me. Shoes I couldn't afford, so I would continue going to school barefoot.

Even though I was barefoot, I felt a little bit better knowing that some of the other kids in my class would come to school without shoes on their feet as well. Since my parents didn't come back to look for me or bring any money to support me, I ended up less fortunate. My cousins would get a dollar fifty for their lunch money, but I would get only seventy-five cents for mine. When break time came, they were able to afford break and after that lunch. As for me, my money would be finished at the break and I would have none for lunch.

You think that because I came from Kingston I would get any special treatment? Think again. I remember one Christmas when everyone had nice clothes to put on because their parents came to visit, brought them nice clothes and shoes, and spent time with them they were so happy with their own parents and gift. No one had time to come see if I was ok. They were too happy. I was the only child who didn't have a visitor, and I was wearing these old shorts that were torn up. I sat on the wall and watched. I can't remember what was going through my mind, but I knew I was sad.

Anyhow, I learned how to live off the land, like how to catch fish, hunt birds, and of course plant crops. The first fish I caught was a frightening experience. I caught a tilapia fish. It weighs about half a pound, so I took it home on about a two-mile journey, and the fish was still alive. It was a freshwater fish, so my cousins and I decided to put it in some salt water, but that didn't kill it. Then we scaled it and gutted it, and the fish was still alive. No, no, no, I wasn't having it, because even without the scales, gills, or guts, we put the fish in water and it would still swim. Then we decided on one final test, which was to put it in the hot frying pan, but the fish was still flipping and flapping. I didn't wait to see if it would die. I ran into the house and said that it was a duppy (ghost) fish.

But of course, whenever I started to feel comfortable, that's when changes came. The first sign of change I saw was one day when I was going to the farm with my cousins. We saw this couple they were white people and they took our pictures and I never saw them again in my life. I said that it was a sign. Because no one but those who knew that place or had been taken there as a guest by someone who came from that district would come there because it was way up in the hills. There were no towns, just mainly houses and farms.

This must have been two years before I left the country and went back to Kingston. My uncle went to America as a farmworker.

I remember when he came back to the country, he brought back pants for us boys it felt good. I don't know what he gave to the girls, as I wasn't an inquisitive child who would want to find out who got what. That's when he brought the little radio with a double cassette tape deck for his parents, my grandpa, and step-grandma. Of course, the radio had to be there for a couple of months before we could even touch it, but when we did, it was like fulfilling a fantasy. So we discovered that we could spit rhymes, and it was fine.

Throughout this period, I was becoming accustomed to the country life. I could feel the difference. My body had adjusted to waking up at five o'clock in the morning to start my day. I could even walk through *Macka* (Thorn) barefoot, like my cousins, without being hurt. I could go the distance without breaking down, managing the same weight as my cousins. I was no longer the frustrated child who would cry and felt helpless as I was before. I had become the real deal. If I fell I would just get up, brush myself off, and kept moving as if nothing had happened.

My cousins, my peers, and I started to be social buddies. We would play games, like marbles. We would draw a circle and throw our marbles, and whoever got the closest to that circle would be the first to start, which gave them the advantage. Also, if a marble went in the circle that would be an automatic win. We would play for rubber bands and even money. Another game we would play was elastic. Someone would toss a rubber band, and others would follow the same pattern. The goal of this game was to keep tossing your rubber bands until it overlapped the other bands that were lying on the floor. Whoever tossed the rubber band that overlapped the others won all the bands that were lying on the floor. If you ended up losing your entire bands you would be out the game.

The Acceptance

After all the crying I had done due to my emotional state, I had to calm down and start to accept the path I was on. It seemed as if I would never see my mother, father, or sister again, so I would have to just accept my grandpa, step-grandma, and cousins as my new family. All I can say is, "What a trip," but just know the experience I had in the country gave me some good knowledge to take on to adulthood, like fending for myself, being self-reliant, disciplined, and hard working.

Even though I had accepted the path that I was on, it had put a permanent scar on me mentally. The intense emotions I had, both bad and good, would stay with me no matter where I go in life. Just remember that I didn't have the freedom of making any independent decisions as a child. This doesn't make me hold any grudges toward anyone in this book or anyone in my life, as I have become an easygoing person who doesn't let most things bother me.

Understanding makes life simple, easier and more exciting in every way. Because I had reached a level of understanding, I was able to accept my path mentally, physically and socially in order to move on to become comfortable. My youth crisis was merely psychological due to the fact that I was separated as a child from my parents. One thing I knew for a fact was that things in my life became plain and simple once I understood how to cope. Another thing was that knowing that my dad had disowned me brought me to an understanding of why I had been treated the way I was treated and possibly why I used to feel the way I did.

I came to realize that I had to settle in as a part of the family. It was hard, but it had to be done. Around the time I was about ten or eleven years old, my uncle came back home. I remember that it was about the same time I was settling in and getting comfortable with my new family. I remember that my step-grandma would cook and all of us would get our dinner. We would all have our own color of enamel plate.

Did I accept the fact that my dad said I wasn't his child but still I needed answers? It started to play out in my mind on how, when, and where I would ask my father why he said I wasn't his child. I didn't ask him until I was about eighteen years old, and his reply was, "Go and ask your mother." I was speechless and offended at the same time, thinking to myself that as a grown man and a father he couldn't give me an explanation. So I didn't even follow up with him about it. However, I did ask my mother and she said the same thing, that I should go ask my father. So I just dropped it and accepted who I was. I was the unwanted child who was abundant because my birth parent didn't have space in their life for me.

Embarrassing moment

Embarrassment is a human emotion of which make a person feel as if he or she isn't good enough. When I was living in the country with my grandfather they were moments that I had that feeling that I wasn't good enough. As much as I tried to fit in it was a struggle. I remember on our journey going to school it was a long journey and we would walk for about 5 miles to get to school if we have to take the long road or we could take the shortcut through the bushes and banana farm which was 2 miles shorter. The journey to school and back home was no walk in the park. If it would rain that's how we would choose our route to school whether it's going to be the long road or the shortcut.

Beyond our house, there was a plantation with acres of bananas that was a farm. Sometime in the morning, the workers would get transported to the farm site for land preparation and banana harvesting. It was a big ten wheeler Mack truck that would take these people to work. As a child one of the truck tires was bigger than us. However, when the truck brought the workers by the banana farm we would set up our self to hitch a ride on the truck as where the truck was returning to was about five hundred yard from our school. The first time I saw my cousins hopped on that big Mack truck I tried and fell and didn't make it. So I had to walk by myself to school while my cousins got to ride on the truck.

    It wasn't cool because when I finally made it to school everyone was there laughing at me asking me what went wrong. I felt so embarrassed moreover I had cuts and bruises. I had never hopped a truck before, but I still didn't quit I did manage to hop that truck and got a ride to school on many occasions. Walking to school in the morning was rough for me because I would be hungry and some days I would spend most of the money before I even got to school. When it was the break I was the child without money to spend.

    I had to wait for lunchtime when the free milk and bun would be shared with the children who couldn't afford to buy lunch. One morning I was at school and my uncle Presho's stepdaughter saw me and ask me to hold her lunch pan for her. I was hungry and she had some fried dumpling in her lunch pan. While she went off and left me holding that lunch pan I took out one of her fried dumplings and ate it without asking her. Her name was Marie; I must say I taught that it was the end of the world by the way she was carrying on over that one fried dumpling that I ate. She created a scene and told her friends that I stole her food that made me felt ashamed. I can't remember taking anything from anyone outside my house after that without asking. It was like everywhere I turned no one wanted me around I felt so bad.

My Cousins and I

Dinnertime used to be interesting; we would do all kinds of things to each other like making a deal that would cause someone to lose their food. The most famous trick was the big-toe trick. One person would ask to take your food and then tell you to lock your big toe with theirs, and while they ate your food, it would transfer through the big toes. Another thing we did while we were eating was that someone would ease their body (pass gas), and this would turn another person off from eating his or her food. Then the one who passed gas would just eat that person's food.

The things my cousins and I did were crazy, and we would do them just to see who was fearless. We would take a hot cup of tea off the wood fire, which was piping hot and then one of us would dare the other one to drink it. Just know that we would accept all challenges. Even if it was to go into a barrel and have someone push it off so we would roll down a hill. What you should know is that the hill that the barrel rolled down wasn't a nice smooth one. There were rocks and cliffs, which caused us to get a burst head or bruises.

We had some huge goats that we would ride like they were donkeys. We would drink milk straight from the cows' or the goats' breasts because there was always a contest between us. Even when we were miles away we still would know each other location. We did this by having a distinct sound, so when one made the sound, the other would answer back with the same identical sound.

Bird hunting was something that I had to learn, as it took skills. First, you would have to know how to make a kia-ta-pol, also known as a slingshot, and your own ca-la-ban, which is a bird catcher. Swimming and climbing trees were skills a child in that district had to learn on his or her own. We also had a dog named Rags, who wouldn't let anyone bother us, even if we were playing with a friend that dog would attack. We had him since he was a puppy. I used to love that dog. We would even feed him when we were eating our dinner.

After dinner, we knew it was our time to hit the kitchen we had to cook the pigs' food, also known as hog feed, as one of our chores. We kids would cook over the wood fire in a five-gallon kerosene pan. I was in the kitchen one evening when a piece of the firewood got stuck under the kerosene pan. I didn't notice and I attempted to fuel the fire by pushing that piece of wood up further into the fire and that whole pan of boiling hot pig food turn over on my back.

Instantly my back had bubbles as tall as six inches. My step-grandma put a whole tin of sweet condensed milk on my back, and I stayed home until it was healed, No one took me to the doctor. We would cook hog feed every evening after Mama cooked dinner. The girls would help clean the dishes and the boys were responsible for cooking the hog feed, among other chores. After that it was bedtime, so we washed our feet and called it a day.

I can't recall how, but I knew that one night we had the cassette tape deck radio to ourselves, *Mon*…. That was a night. Dada and Mama were nowhere around so we had a blast. *Yah Mon*, we were riding the rhythm, spitting rhymes, and having fun. Then my uncle just appeared out of nowhere. It was a night to remember. The lyrics I was chatting were very explicit, so when he showed up we all took exits that we didn't even know existed. I think that we were recording also, because it was a double-deck cassette tape recorder, while one side played the other side recorded. I remembered running outside and down the road away from my uncle, and sleeping under the house (in the cellar) that night.

Also as a farmer, my grandfather would produce a little marijuana and tobacco for his personal use. So while my cousins and I was having fun we got curious. We would go into our grandfather bedside table drawer where he would hide a secret stash of marijuana and smoke it. It seemed that smoking paper and dry leaf as practice worked out for us because we didn't get any dizziness or had any suspicious behavior to get caught.

The Secret Passage My Utopia

I had a secret passage that I used to enter into and out of the cellar. Everything was going well for a while because no one else knew of it but me. My step-grandmother would put special produce in the cellar, and it was also the storage for my grandfather's produce that he would sell to the market vendors. The cellar was always under lock and key and that door would not be open without the presence of Mama or Dada, as they would supervise what went in or came out of the cellar. But I had that secret entrance, and I would go in and out as I liked.

Of course, all good things must come to an end. I had it good; the cellar was like my utopia. So as long as I was the only one who knew about that secret passage, things were good. I would enter and exit as I liked, ate and fill my stomach or just went there to relax. There was always something good inside the cellar, locked away from us kids, like ripe bananas and other delicious fruits and vegetable. Whenever a special bunch of bananas was yielded on the farm, it wouldn't be sold to the *Higgler* (vendors) at the market.

My grandfather had lots of things on the farm: fruits like avocado, jackfruit, apples, and guava, just to name a few, and there were many more. But the plantains and bananas were like the classic, especially the rear and unique types of banana. For one, there were the butter bananas. Those would get stored in the cellar to ripen, and then Mama would take them herself to the market to sell. In that way, she would make more money by selling it direct the customers without using the vendors.

So, what I would do is enter through my secret passage and have a feast, and then cover my tracks so I didn't get caught. I would ensure that no banana skins were left behind, or I would picked a banana from the end and not the middle, then put that hand of banana that I ate from in the bottom of the pile of bananas. Sometimes there were six-fingers on a hand of banana and I would just have to eat the whole hand and take the skins with me.

It crossed my mind whether she would miss a whole hand of bananas, but she never asked any questions, so I continued to do it. It was my getaway place, especially when I was hungry, and at that age, I could consume a good portion of food. So when I would go to my escape place under the cellar to enjoy those ripe bananas, I would be content. I would even fall asleep sometimes when I ate my tummy full. But as always, nothing lasts forever.

The biggest mistake I made at that time was when I thought I could trust someone. My cousin Merrick Hutchinson he and I were close, so I invited him in on my little secret, thinking he would keep my secret while enjoying the ripe bananas with me. I took him with me under the cellar through my secret passage into my utopia. We ate so many ripe bananas we couldn't move. We sat and talked and laughed until we realized that we had to get out of the cellar.

I stood up and got ready to walk off, but after having so much to eat; I suddenly stopped and looked at him. He was looking back at me in shock, wondering what was wrong. But it took a few seconds for either of us to react to the abrupt, intense look that we had shared.

I said to him, "I can't move."

He looked at me and asked, "Why?"

I said, "I am stuffed."

He chuckled, and I was in a very tense position. Then he realized that I was just standing still, motionless and stiff. At that point, I had no idea what was going through his mind. All I knew was that I couldn't move, and I needed to get out of the cellar before anyone noticed we were missing.

I turned to him and said, "You go first."

He said, "No, I'm not leaving you. We are going together."

I said, "I can't move."

He asked why.

I said, "I want to *doo-doo* (pooped)"

He said, "OK, let's go, and you can go use the latrine."

I said, "I naw go mek it," (I'm not going to make it) so again we gave each other the look.

Now, what will I do? Was going through my mind, knowing that if I doo-doo up myself it was going to be a big disgrace to me. Knowing already that I was the child that didn't fit in and that they just wanted another thing to use and make fun of me with. This was going through my head, how they would call me shit-up pants, and as a child that was mentally damaging.

I had to move quickly and bravely without thinking of the outcome and of course, what I did neither of us saw it coming. The cellar was a good size, and it had powdered dirt as the flooring. Also, all my granddad's best farm tools were kept locked away safely in there. I looked and saw the farm tools in a corner where we were. Without hesitation, I moved toward the farm tools, took the digging fork, and dug a hole in the cellar, pulled my pants and briefs down, and *doo-doo* (pooped) in that hole and covered it up. That day I decided that no one was going to call me shit-up. I put the fork back; set the place up as it was, then we left the cellar. Things were back in order you wouldn't have any idea that we did something wrong unless someone told you.

I think I went a little too far with my cousin. He wasn't having any part of that. This is why I always said that if you are doing anything that you don't want anyone to find out do it yourself. Then the only ones who will know are you and God because the only way someone else will know is if you told them. I thought that everything was good. I fed him and brought him in on my secret, so we were good. No, it wasn't like that. Somehow he hid away from me and went to Mama and told her what happened in the cellar.

I was sitting with the rest of my cousins, acting normal, and there came Mama, calling me, which was unusual. She took me to the back of the house and stood at the door of the cellar. My heart was beating very fast, as I was trying to keep calm because she couldn't have known anything about what happened. She reached for her keys and opened the door of the cellar, and she turned to me and said,

"Where did you do it?" I acted like I had no idea what she was talking about.

She didn't waste any time playing this game with me. The look on her face was so angry. Without a second question to me, she called my cousin Merrick. Here he came. I was so disappointed. Mama just asked the little snitch where, and he pointed out the location. She then turned and looked at me. I knew that playing stubborn with her was done. She was mad. She had me dig it out. Ever since then, I find it very hard to trust anyone.

Was I wrong or was I right to did what I did that's the question I kept asking myself. But at the moment I had to think quickly and on the other hand, I had already let my cousin in on the secret of my hiding place so there was never a doubt that my cousin would keep this a secret. But this just proves to me that whenever you are doing anything make sure that it is the right thing are if it's something wrong do it by yourself.

My Utopia secret passage

A Hungry boy

One night we had fried dumplings for dinner it was delicious and not enough for me. So when it was bedtime I was still hungry. I remember that mama had a few leftover fried dumplings covered up on the table in the dining room; this was right next to the room where we slept. I sneaked out into the dining room where she had the fried dumplings took one and head back to where I was sleeping. But there was only one problem the fried dumpling was so crunchy and delicious no matter how I tried to be quiet the crunching sound was so loud. Mama must have gotten curious after hearing that crunchy sound knowing that everyone should be in bed and the house should be quiet unless it was a rat pulling something.

I must have been a fool to think that I would get away with this. Because, she blast in the room straight to my area where I was sleeping on the floor behind the door. I was on my right side covered from head to toe and I heard the footsteps coming. Then the footstep stop and I felt someone touched me I was frantic as I knew that I was going to be in a lot of trouble if I got caught with that fried dumpling knowing I didn't ask for it. "Dane what you eating," Mama asked. I swallow and took my time, turn to her and said "nothing".

She turned the lamp up because we would turn the lamp down in the house when it was bedtime. She shouted at the top of her voice as she knew I was lying and she started to get angry. She started accusing me without any proof or evidence that I was guilty of the crime she was accusing me of. As all she heard was a sound. Right on the attack shouting "where is it, where is it" I couldn't even answer her as I was afraid and nervous because this is not good. What am I going to do I had no defense and I still had the fried dumpling on me and there was nowhere I could throw it are hiding it.

So I move slowly again swallow my saliva kept looking at her at this time I was standing up. I finally said in a frightened and scared way "what ma?" she replied to me "how you mean what?" she knew the crunchy sound so she said "the dumpling". I said, "I don't have any dumpling" at this time her anger became a rage. I started to shake; trembling as I knew if she found that fried dumpling on me the beating I would get would be merciless. Because this was stealing and stealing wasn't acceptable in that house.

I know I better not get caught because this is a serious matter. Then she walked away to make sure that what she is accusing me of was true. She heads to the living room to check on the table where she had covered up the fried dumplings because she knows how much dumplings she had left as she would use it for dada's breakfast the next morning. After she had counted the dumplings she got even madder, stamping her feet on the wooden floor shouting and saying all kinds of swearing words. On the way back to me she is now sure of how many dumplings she left and one was missing.

At this time the whole house was awake by the way she was carrying on even my cousins started to look worried. Even though she knew the dumpling was missing she wasn't able to find the dumpling on me.

But she knows how many dumplings she had and she was so determined to find it on me. She went back out into the dining room and return again, now she was more certain that one of the dumplings were missing as she stamped her feet on the wooden floor I could feel it shake and I could also feel her anger.

Let me say at this time if I could vanish I would, however, I knew that as long as she didn't find the fried dumpling that was missing on me, I would be fine. So she started to search me by shaken out my clothing, pulling apart my bed and having me opening my mouth over and over again. But as the search continued and there was no dumpling insight I became a bit calmer as I watched her search where there was no dumpling to be found. She pulled out the entire drawer from the dresser because I was sleeping right in front of the dresser on the floor behind the door.

Also, there was a bag which was hanged on the door she went through that bag thoroughly and didn't found the fried dumpling. My bed was made out of *(Crocus bag)* also known as burlap bag stuff with dry trash so it was easy to move. She also took my bed up and shook it out in search for the missing fried dumpling. By now all my cousins up gathered to one side of the room watching the whole mess about to unfold. I had to keep my cool making sure that mama didn't pick up any weakness that would make her pressure me any more than she is doing.

The question still lies where is the fried dumpling? As she was sure that one was missing from the batch she had on the table in the dining room. Of course, she isn't going out looking like a fool knowing that she is right so she had to find it. But after she searches everywhere and still couldn't find the fried dumpling she looked at me with a straight face. She had realized that there was one spot left to search and that was my hands. She said "stretch out tour hands" I pause, then quickly stretch one of my hand out and held the sheet with the other hand. Then she said again "let me see the next hand" so I put the sheet in the hand that I stretch out first and then I stretch the next hand out.

Disappointed, she knew that she was right but there was no evidence there to support her. She went back to her room and I fix back my bed and went back to sleep. Now I know that I better finish eating the rest of the fried dumpling because if anyone saw me with it in the morning it would be double trouble. I just got lucky that night because when she went after anyone she usually got them and get them good.

So I was able to escape another embarrassing moment. You know what, I took a risk and learned from it. I learned never to take anything that doesn't belong to me without asking permission. Because the fear that mama drove in me looking for that fried dumpling was a fear I don't ever want to feel again. Other times came when I was hungry and I knew to wait until the next meal was served.

The Clash

My uncle was home now and he did some farming because when you came back home, the elders would start you off in life with something to make a living. They would help you to get back on your feet. This was their custom, to start you over again by giving you land and some seeds or whatever crop they could give you to plant on the land. My uncle got Irish potatoes and yam heads to start over with. He planted about one and a half bags of Irish potatoes. It looked good, and I remembered they were saying to him that it would yield well, meaning that he would make a good profit.

I believed that Uncle Max and Dada couldn't agree because Max was the last child, and he was young and carefree. On top of that, he carried a gun into the house, and Dada wasn't into that lifestyle. Even though they weren't on the same terms most of the time, Dada still loved and cared for his son. But Dada would only act mad at him because he didn't want Uncle Max to waste his youth. This showed when Dada bought a car. It was a Vauxhall sedan, and he only trusted Uncle Max to drive it. Also, the car was one of the few things that brought them closer together, because Max wasn't a huge fan of farming.

I, on the other hand, had a few seeds of Irish potato, and I made my ca-la-ban, which was a small cage used to catch birds that flew down on the ground to pick up corn or bird feed that's placed under the ca-la-ban, which is tripped by a piece of card on a split stick. Now came the revelation between Dane and Max (I don't know his full name because all of us as kids would call him Uncle Max). I went to check my ca-la-ban to see if I had caught any birds. When I got there, I saw that my ca-la-ban was damaged and bird feathers were everywhere, so I immediately accused Uncle Max. I can't remember why I accused him, but I did, and no one could tell me otherwise. *Mon*, I was furious.

To get revenge, I went over to his potato farm, which was near where I set my ca-la-ban. Oh boy. I should have thought twice because without any evidence I just went and cut down all his Irish potatoes. I have no idea how he knew it was me, but he found out—and that was just the beginning. I remember he was about twenty-seven years old, and I was about ten years old. I thought I was mad; he made my anger look like a joke. One thing I can say is that on that day it was the fastest I have ever run. Uncle Max came down from the house, cursing and swearing that he was going to kill me.

I was an idiot to stand there arguing with him until I said the wrong thing, which must have hit a nerve and made him furious. He tried to grab me, and I took off and he pursued. I can remember that I ran and I ran. I must have run over three miles because we were both tired. But he built up the extra energy because he wanted revenge, and he did get it. When he finally caught me, even with our tiredness, he started beating me. He beat and he beat me. I swear if he hadn't been tired I might have ended up in the hospital. Thinking about it now Dada, my grandpa, who would always come to my rescue, was nowhere to be found.

I guess this was my faith and there wasn't any mercy this time. As somethings just are the way they are and one has to face their demons no matter what. This was very shocking I must have been acting impulsively to not think that there wasn't going to be any consequence to my action, for cutting down my uncle potato farm. This storyline is to advise you to think before you act in any circumstances because you must remember that you aren't the only one who has a move in the game.

Another thing is that you shouldn't be quick to judge as haste makes waste in some cases and I am a prime example of that. It got me a beat down in a way that couldn't imagine.But a lesson I learned is that I won't be an example of irrational thinking ever again.

Conclusion

Life lessons are what you learn in your everyday life from the actions you take or the actions that happen in your surroundings. What I understand is that life is not what it seems to be all the time. Also, in order to achieve what you want, there is a price to pay. The people who are closest to you are the ones who hurt you the most. You can also be hurt knowing that you aren't in a position to help the one you care for so much. Life comes with its challenges, and you learn from each experience.

Also, growing up in that environment shadowed me from expressing myself. This would follow me through my teenage years, being a bit shy, which held me back from my full potential because I believed that the adults would act in the same fashion everywhere, even when I got back to Kingston. This had a significant impact on my life, whenever I got an opportunity, to show my talent I would hold back thinking that I would be out of line. As I mentioned earlier about my love for the performing arts, my opportunity to be a performer would come when I got back to Kingston. Whenever I would go to do an audition, I wouldn't perform to my fullest potential because there were all adults around me and I was very careful of what I would say or how I would act. As an adult now, I see how my fearfulness hindered me from landing a role.

How would I know that it was because my dad disowned me that I used to feel alone? He is deceased now, so I guess I will never know the answer to that or even the reason why he treated me the way he did when I went to stay with him. I had a humble spirit, and that carried me through my rage and when I was feeling low. I didn't make a living out of the performing arts, but I had gotten the opportunity to be a part of some great projects. I learned how to cope so I could get through the difficulties that I faced in life. This brings me to the place of accepting things for what they are and learning from them. By facing my demons and not running away from my responsibilities, I realize that even if I didn't do what I was supposed to do, I wouldn't get off from doing it, it would just push back my work and made it harder for me. Just like when I had to go back for water until I had carried the same amount as my cousins.

Glossary

Bwoy .... Boy

Ca-la-ban ……………….. A pyramid-like cage built and set as a trap to catch birds

Cut .... In Jamaica this means moving from one location to another swiftly.

Dada .... Grandfather

Dolly house .... Kids playing house when their parents aren't home

Doo-doo .... Poop

Yuh................................. You

Duppy............................. Ghost Spirit

Eh .... Yes - as in answer a call

Ehm .... Him

Kingstonian .... A person who is born in the Kingston City

Kia-ta-pol .... Slingshot

Macka............................. Thorns

Mama............................. Grandmother

Mek	Make
Mi	Me
Mon	Man
Naw	Not going to
Skulling	Skipping school without permission
Spliff	A marijuana cigarette
Tenement yard	multifamily housing arrangement consisting of many substandard dwellings packed closely on a single plot of land; dwellings often share resources such as running water and toilets

CPSIA information can be obtained
at www.ICGtesting.com
Printed in the USA
BVHW041832240321
603359BV00017B/642